STRATHCLYDE TRACTION

Colin J. Howat

AMBERLEY

First published 2016

Amberley Publishing
The Hill, Stroud
Gloucestershire, GL5 4EP

www.amberley-books.com

Copyright © Colin J. Howat, 2016

The right of Colin J. Howat to be identified as
the Author of this work has been asserted in
accordance with the Copyrights, Designs and
Patents Act 1988.

ISBN 978 1 4456 6284 8 (print)
ISBN 978 1 4456 6285 5 (ebook)

British Library Cataloguing in Publication Data.
A catalogue record for this book is available from
the British Library.

Typesetting by Amberley Publishing.
Printed in the UK.

Introduction

Strathclyde Traction is mainly based around the former Strathclyde Regional Council area of the west of Scotland. The old counties within Scotland were replaced with new regional areas created by the government, one of which was the Strathclyde region, which existed until 1996. What, then, were the main reasons for the major change leading to the formation of the Strathclyde region? After the severe cuts arising from the Doctor Beeching review of 1963, Glasgow lost two major stations. As well as losing Glasgow St Enoch and Glasgow Buchanan Street stations, many connecting lines were lost, including the Argyle Line between Kelvinhaugh Junction and Rutherglen. Further cuts towards the end of the 1960s were on the cards, but fortunately the Labour government was re-elected in 1964. This stopped further closures and the transport act of 1968 helped further. The transport minister at the time, Barbara Castle, was able to halt some of the madness. It was harder for British Rail to close lines, as complicated public close-down procedures were introduced. By January 1969, the new act came into force. The main provisions affecting the railways were the creation of executives and passenger authorities to take over the running more directly of the railways within their designated areas. The authorities were to be made up of councillors from the various local authorities in the area, while the executives were to be the operators of public transport, in the most part taking the lead role in regard to subsidising local railways. Following further consultations, PTAs/PTEs were established under the act. For Strathclyde, the act established the Greater Glasgow PTE initially, which started officially on 1 June 1973. This newly created body would also have responsibility for the Glasgow Underground, as well as bus and rail services. Part of the act introduced funding from the government for railways, in the form of a subsidy. This included help for lines that were running at a loss but that were deemed socially and economically necessary. However, for any subsidy to be paid, certain conditions had to be agreed. This included financial help for lines deemed uneconomical.

In conjunction to this, Strathclyde region was then formed by merging the city of Glasgow with the outlying areas of Ayrshire, Buteshire, Dumbartonshire, Lanarkshire, Renfrewshire, Stirlingshire and parts of Argyll. The first visual sign of the Scottish PTE's influence on the railways was during 1977, when the symbol GG, standing for 'Greater Glasgow', started to appear on the sides of units. Later the word 'Transclyde' was added and units had the Strathclyde graphic vinyl applied with a map of Scotland, which included the area of Strathclyde highlighted within it. By the start of the 1980s, it was agreed by the selected bodies of the Greater Glasgow PTE and British Rail that the ageing fleet of blue trains (Class 303s) would have to be upgraded. This then led to a refurbishment programme, whereby a designated fifty out of the ninety-one Class 303 fleet were upgraded. This was carried out between 1984 and 1990. When these units emerged from Glasgow Works, the following main visual modifications were completed: they were painted orange, had interconnecting gangway doors between each coach, new hopper-style windows and new seating arrangements. Some of the Class 101 and 107 units would also later be painted in the familiar Strathclyde orange livery, with the Strathclyde map on each coach. Some un-refurbished Class 303 and 311 units were also painted in orange livery, but left with the old seats and windows.

As stated earlier, Strathclyde PTE started to change train liveries from 1977. An early experimental white and blue livery was applied to various Class 101 DMUs, but was later deemed unsuccessful. This was shortlived and fell out of favour by the early 1980s. At this period there were also operational changes. The new Class 303 units that came out of Glasgow Works had also become driver-only units under what was termed the Strathclyde Manning Arrangements (SMA). This effectively did away with the guards on these trains. Most stations within the Strathclyde area were also fitted with mirrors and CCTV to assist this type of operation. However, there was quite a bit of industrial unrest, with strike action taken on numerous occasions until agreement was reached with the unions. Certain other 303 units were transferred to Crewe Electric depot in England, where they were used in and around the Manchester and Crewe areas. These units were never painted in the Strathclyde orange livery. Some of the Shields-based Class 311 units did receive the orange livery as well but were never refurbished. By 1986 many electric units were in Strathclyde orange, and the new Class 318 units ordered for the Ayrshire electrification scheme came straight into service with the orange livery and maps. By 1998 the tired orange livery was being replaced by the new maroon and cream livery. Four Class 303 units also received this livery. From 2009 the new ScotRail saltire livery also began to replace this as well.

As a schoolboy in the early 1970s, I took very few railway pictures. However, by 1977, as a sixteen-year-old lad, my interest in travel was expanding. Previously I had been restricted by school studies and other matters. However, when I got to the summer of 1977, I bought a Strathclyde Railrover pass. This allowed me to explore most of the Strathclyde area. The following year I was able to cover most of the remaining areas, as I had purchased a Freedom Of Scotland pass that allowed me unlimited travel all over Scotland and as far south as Carlisle. I do regret that, on both these annual adventures, very little photography was undertaken. The opposite then occurred when I attended college in Glasgow between 1978 and 1980, where I studied general photography and, when time allowed, I began building up my own railway photographic collection in addition to my college work. In the summer of 1979, during my summer break from college, I again purchased a Strathclyde Railrover pass and, this time armed with a Praktica Nova 35-mm camera with black-and-white film, I ventured around the Strathclyde area once again. Later In 1981, I again purchased another Freedom Of Scotland pass and travelled extensively all over Scotland. Much of my early work was in black and white but, from 1981 onwards, I have mostly shot colour-negative 35-mm and colour-slide films, with the odd large-format films used as well. This included carrying about a large Arca 4x5 large-format camera and a 120-mm Hasselblad camera. From 2002 I joined the digital bandwagon and, apart from the odd slide film, most of my work is now digital. This has certainly reduced my storage requirements.

Thinking back to my seventies travels, a few of the lines that I had travelled over at the time have now gone. This includes High Street to Bridgeton Cross, Balloch Pier, Dalry to Kilmarnock and the Paisley Canal to Kilmacolm branch. The Balloch branch was singled in 1977 and the Milngavie branch was partly singled again in the early 1980s. Single lead junctions became popular with the civil engineers and helped to reduce costs at busy junctions, but have caused severe congestion in today's modern railway. In recent years, this has been accepted and double lead junctions have been reintroduced at Busby Junction, where the Barrhead and East Kilbride lines diverge, and at Newton, where the Kirkhill and Argyle line services diverge. What of the future? The Airdrie to Bathgate line reopened in December 2010, but again basic signalling only has been provided and other lines have reopened. On the negative side, Hyndland depot closed with the opening of Yoker depot in in 1987. This area has again been replaced by the usual housing developments. Some freight spurs have also come and gone, and it looks as if the Waterside branch south of Ayr is doomed to be lifted in the near future. Coal traffic has also declined, due to falling demand from the large power stations in England. Similarly, within Scotland itself, coal traffic between Hunterston Clyde Port and Longannet power station ceased from the end of March 2016. For me personally, the closure of the Kilmacolm line was the biggest mistake. It closed in January 1983 with no thought given to making it part of the main Ayrshire electrification scheme, which started up in September 1986. Worse was to follow as, shortly after the line was closed, the track beyond Paisley Canal was lifted and the land was later sold off to a developer in 1987, who built approximately twenty houses over the track area just beyond Paisley Canal station and the yard leading to it. By the early 1990s it was recognised by various bodies, including the Greater Glasgow PTE, that a bad mistake had been made. An hourly Sprinter service was then reintroduced from 1991 from Glasgow Central to Paisley Canal, with two new stations at Dumbreck and Paisley Hawkhead. In May 1992, old 101 DMUs were brought back to give a half-hourly service. These units also ran to Whifflet and Barrhead. Eventually, from October 2000, all first-generation DMUs were withdrawn and replaced by Class 156 units. The 101s were transferred to Newton Heath Manchester and some of them continued in service as late as 2005. Some have also been preserved. However, despite these improvements, no attempt has been made to extend the line between Paisley Canal and Elderslie, mainly due to the costs involved in buying back the land sold off for a housing estate. The station building is now a restaurant. Much disruption in the intervening years from 1983 until 2012 was caused between Paisley Gilmour Street and Shields Junction outside Glasgow, due to freight-train failures, and I personally had the misfortune of being stuck behind many both going to and from Glasgow Central. Eventually, as part of the proposed Glasgow Airport scheme, a middle track was reinstated between Shields Junction and Paisley Gilmour Street from 2012, which has made a vast improvement.

In 1992 a small crossing loop at Crookston on the Paisley Canal was provided and, in 2012, the single line was electrified. However, this is another line where the single line constraints limit any operational flexibility. Bridgeton Central, on the east side of Glasgow, was an ex-Caledonian terminus and closed in November 1979. It was retained as a cleaning depot until 1987. It was replaced by a new station called Bridgeton, situated approximately 500 yards away on the newly reopened Argyle line. New services ran between Lanark and Motherwell on the south side of the river, while Dalmuir and Dumbarton Central, north of the Clyde, connected the new Bridgeton station to them. This proved to one of the better decisions made by the Strathclyde Passenger Transport Executive, although BR Scottish Region deserve credit as well for not allowing the Argyle Line to be turned into a roadway, which had been proposed in the early 1970s. What of the future? The Scottish parliament has invested quite substantially in projects in the east. This includes the new Borders Rail Link, the tram system, the second Forth Road Bridge and a new £30-million airport station at Gogar for Edinburgh Airport. The elected SNP administration at Holyrood pulled the plug on the Glasgow Airport link in 2010, stating lack of finance, so passengers will still have to travel by rail to Paisley Gilmour Street and change into a bus link to the airport. It looks as if other lines within the Strathclyde area that are operated by diesel Sprinters will eventually be electrified. Glasgow to Shotts seems to be one of the favourites, with Glasgow to Barrhead, Kilmarnock and East Kilbride on the horizon. However, due to the ongoing financial constraints, this does not seem likely to happen for at least another ten years. Like the rest of the UK, Scotland's railways, particularly Strathclyde, have seen increasing numbers of passenger traffic but freight traffic is virtually nil at present. Who knows – perhaps Glasgow St Enoch station may be reopened in the future as part of a cross-city route between Glasgow and Edinburgh. Now who would have thought that in 1966?

Depot Codes:

AY – Ayr
CD – Crewe Diesel
CE – Crewe Electric
CK – Corkerhill Glasgow
CL – Colas Rugby
ED – Eastfield Glasgow
DR – DRS Carlisle
DY – Etches Park Derby
FL – Freightliner Leeds
GB – GB Railfreight Doncaster
GD – Gateshead
GW – Shields Depot Glasgow
HA – Haymarket
HM – Healey Mills
HN – Hamilton Depot
HY – Hyndland Glasgow
HA – Headquarters (BR)
IS – Inverness
KD – Carlisle Kingmoor (BR)
LO – Longsight Manchester
NL – Nelville Hill Leeds
SF – Stratford London
TI – Tinsley Sheffield
TO – Toton Nottingham
TE – Thornaby Tees
WN – Willesden London

Strathclyde Transport map, as depicted on the side of a Class 311 EMU in Airdrie sidings. Most Class 303 and 311 units had this map vinyl adorned on the side of each coach. Taken in May 1984.

View of Glasgow Central station concourse. This shows the old arrival and destination boards, which were manually moved up and down by a railman. The manual boarding system was eventually replaced by an electronic system from May 1985. LED boards thence took over from 2004. Taken in July 1976.

Six-car 107 DMU at the old Platform 13 Glasgow Central. These units were working the 18.15 service to Largs. At this time, both units would have been allocated to Hamilton depot. Platform 13 became Platform 15 when station refurbishment took place in 2010. However, the old car park was removed to allow the upgrading to take place. Taken in August 1975.

No. 303058 (HY) at Balloch Pier, having just arrived with a train from Bridgeton Central. This station closed to passengers in 1986. This was due to a review of station operations by Strathclyde Passenger Executive. However, it was also due to the earlier withdrawal of the steamer service from Balloch Pier to Loch Lomond, which ended in 1981. The steamer boat *Maid of the Loch* is currently being refurbished and may take to the waters again in the future. Taken in July 1979.

Three-car 107 takes the dive under the junction at Elderslie No. 2 signal box with a Glasgow–Kilmacolm train. This line went under the main Glasgow–Ayr line towards Cart Junction. Here the tracks further divided, with one line heading towards Kilmacolm and the other towards Dalry via Kilbarchan. The Kilbarchan Loop line finally closed in 1972, and Kilmacolm in 1983. Taken in July 1979.

Three-car 116 from Hamilton depot at Cart Junction with a Kilmacolm–Glasgow Central via Paisley Canal service. At one time, this junction had six tracks. By 1973 it had been reduced to one single track with only an hourly service to and from Kilmacolm. This service was eventually withdrawn in January 1983. Taken in July 1979.

No. 45123 (TI) at Glasgow Central with the 10.50 service to Nottingham via Kilmarnock, Dumfries and
Carlisle. This was a remnant of the old Thames–Clyde expresses that ran from Glasgow St Enoch to London
St Pancras. These locomotives, with classes 40 and 46, were banned from Glasgow Central from 1981 after a
number of derailments outside the station in the jungle area. Taken in October 1979.

Bridgeton Central with a mixture of Class 303s and DMU Gloucester railcar No. 55005 (ED) on a
driver-trainer. This station closed to passengers on commencement of the new Argyle line in November 1979.
It was still used as a carriage-cleaning facility until 1987, when the last ECS departed. These cleaning duties
thence transferred to a new depot at Yoker on the north-west side of Glasgow. Taken in October 1979.

No. 27211 (ED) at the head of old-style push-and-pull service at Glasgow Queen Street with a service for Edinburgh. The 27s replaced Swindon Inter City DMUs from 1972 but were replaced by Class 47s and Mk3 stock from September 1979. Taken in October 1979.

No. 40067 (HM) backs on to coaches in Platform 7 at Glasgow Queen Street to work the 09.25 service to Aberdeen. Class 40 locos were common at this time and worked not only Aberdeen trains but also services to Perth and Inverness, including the overnight sleeper to Inverness. Taken in October 1979.

DMU Class No. 101222 (ED) arrives at Platform 3 Glasgow Queen Street with a train from Falkirk Grahamston. Taken in October 1979.

Bridge Street outside Glasgow Central. On the left is six-car 126 DMU with a service to Ayr while, on the right, a Class 87 heads an Inter City service for London Euston. The Class 126 DMUs were finally withdrawn from service in 1983. The Class 87s worked with Virgin West Coast until 2004. Some are still in use abroad. Taken in June 1980.

No. 83010 (CE) brings in ECS to Glasgow Central. These coaches would form a Glasgow–Liverpool and Manchester service. An additional six coaches would be coupled up at Carstairs, which would have departed from Edinburgh Waverley. Taken in August 1979.

Six-car 101, unit 176 (HN) leading at Drybridge between Kilmarnock and Barassie with the 1935 Glasgow Central–Ayr via Kilmarnock service. This was the first experimental Strathclyde PTE livery in white but was deemed unsuccessful. It was later replaced by the familiar orange livery. Taken in August 1978.

No. 40096 (LO) passes Newton with a freightliner service from Glasgow Gushetfaulds terminal to London Brent terminal. This loco was withdrawn from traffic in December 1983 and broken up at Doncaster works by May 1986. Taken in May 1980.

Six-car 314, 210 unit trailing (HY) at Newton station with a Motherwell–Dalmuir via Blantyre and Singer service. The steelworks on the left is long gone, being replaced by a station car park and houses. Taken in May 1980.

Three-car 107, unit 150 (HN) at Bridge Of Weir station with the 14.07 Glasgow Central–Kilmacolm service. The destination board incorrectly reads, 'Kilmarnock'. Taken in November 1980.

EMU Class No. 303023 (GW) at Motherwell with a service to Milngavie. This was one of the few 303 units that received the Strathclyde maroon-and-cream livery. Taken in August 1999.

Glasgow Works open day sees ex-North British steam loco No. 673 *Maude*, owned by the Scottish Railway Preservation Society based at Bo'ness, arriving at the works with a shuttle service to and from a headshunt outside the works. Note the Red Road flats in left background. These flats were at one time the tallest in Western Europe. However, they were all eventually demolished by October 2015. Taken in June 1981.

Six-car 303, unit 063 (HY) leading arrives at Barnhill with a Springburn–Balloch Central via Singer service. At this time, there was a half-hourly service, with certain services extended to Balloch Pier. This unit was not included in the orange livery refurbishment programme and was withdrawn from service in May 1990. Taken in June 1981.

HST at Glasgow Queen Street with the 09.45 Sunday service to London King's Cross via Edinburgh. This service called at Falkirk High, Polmont, Linlithgow and Haymarket prior to Edinburgh. This through service was withdrawn in 1989. The power cars on this occasion were Nos 43088 and 43089, both at this time allocated to Edinburgh Craigentinny depot. Taken in July 1981.

Six-car 105 DMU, unit 375 leading (HA), arrives in Glasgow Queen Street with a service from Falkirk Grahamston. Class 105s were all withdrawn from Scottish services by 1986. Taken in March 1981.

No. 82001 (LO) near Shields Junction with a car train from Luton to Elderslie car terminal north of Johnstone. The Class 82 worked the train as far as Paisley Loop, where a diesel loco took over for the short distance from Paisley to Elderslie. The cars and vans were distributed from a massive car park adjacent to the old Linwood factory. This loco was withdrawn from traffic in July 1983 and scrapped at Vic Berry's, Leicester, by March 1985. Taken in August 1981.

Six-car 126 DMU at Benhar Junction, east of Shotts. At this time, Class 126s on the Shotts line were virtually unheard of. This six-car replaced a failed three-car 107. It worked from Glasgow Central to Shotts, then ECS to Benhar Junction, where it reversed and then formed a Shotts–Motherwell service, before running ECS back to Corkerhill depot. Taken in August 1981.

Springburn station. In the foreground is a three-car 101, having just arrived with a service from Cumbernauld, and, in the bay platforms, an assortment of Class 303s on local workings. In 1992 the Cumbernauld–Springburn service was extended to Glasgow Queen Street via Eastfield Loop. Then in 1995 a new spur called the Cowlairs Chord was installed between Springburn station and Cowlairs North Junction, thereby allowing Cumbernauld services a direct route to Glasgow Queen Street. Since 2014, electric services have taken over more routes and generally now run from Cumbernauld to Dalmuir, reversing in Springburn station. Taken in August 1981.

Six-car 303, unit 031 leading (HY), emerges from Dalmuir twin tunnels towards Dalreoch station with a Helensburgh Central–Airdrie via Singer service. Note the Balloch branch in the background. This branch was singled in 1977. Taken in August 1981.

No. 25146 (KD) at Corkerhill depot, having just arrived with fuel tanks from Grangemouth Oil terminal. Scottish depots now receive their fuel deliveries mainly by road. Taken in March 1982.

HST passing Polmadie depot with a diverted Glasgow Central–London King's Cross via Shotts and Edinburgh service. This service was diverted away from Glasgow Queen Street, due to engineering works in the Falkirk area. Taken in April 1982.

No. 26034 (IS) at Glasgow Central, having just arrived with the 13.30 service from Stranraer Harbour. These locos had just recently replaced the Class 126 DMUs. Taken in May 1982.

Neilston sidings with an assortment of Class 303s. These units were stabled here regularly in connection with football at Hamden Park. The sidings were closed in the mid-1980s, leaving a small turn-round siding. However, due to its size, Class 380s cannot use it. Taken in May 1982.

No. 46032 (GD) at Croftfoot station with a football special from Edinburgh to Kings Park. Diesels on specials to Hampden Park are now a thing of the past. Taken in May 1982.

Six-car 116/107 DMU combination at Crookston box with a special day excursion from Ayr to Corkerhill station, in connection with the papal visit to Bellahouston Park, Glasgow. Taken in June 1982.

Three-car 107 DMU, east of Paisley Canal station, with the 11.03 Kilmacolm–Glasgow Central service. Note the Western SMT bus garage adjacent to the line, which is now closed. Taken in June 1982.

No. 37073 (TE) at Corkerhill No. 1 signalbox with a special from Falkirk Grahamston to Corkerhill station, again in connection with the papal visit. Taken in June 1982.

Nos 37084 and 37156 (Both ML) with Class 20175 (ED) providing banking assistance on the rear at Mossend Yard with a loaded ore train from Hunterston to Ravenscraig No 2. Taken in May 1982.

Elderslie Junction. In the foreground is a six-car 101 with the 09.03 Kilmacolm–Glasgow Central service. In the background, a six-car 126 is heading south with the 09.00 Glasgow Central–Girvan service. Also in the Up Loop is a six-car 107 on ECS from Glasgow Central to Ardrossan Harbour. In the Down Loop lie cars and vans that were brought up from Luton for distribution to various dealerships. The cars and vans were stored in a massive car park adjacent to the former Linwood factory. Taken in June 1982.

No. 85023 (CE) at Mossend Yard with cement empty tanks to Clunie, near Blackburn. This loco was scrapped at MC Metals of Glasgow in 1990. Taken in May 1982.

Nine-car 107 at Coatbridge Central, with a day excursion to Ayr. This was for various schools in the Coatbridge area. All units at this time were allocated to Ayr depot. These excursions continued until 2009. Taken in May 1983.

No. 25178 (CD) at Paisley Gilmour Street with a southbound coal train from Mossend to Falkland yard service. This loco was scrapped at Vic Berry's yard, Leicester, by March 1989. Taken in May 1982.

A six-car 107 passes Paisley Signalling Centre with a Largs–Glasgow Central service. This signalling centre closed in 2008 and all work was transferred to the West of Scotland Signalling Centre, based in Springburn on the north side of Glasgow. Taken in May 1983.

No. 81016 (GW) at Greenock Central with a day excursion from Gourock to Oxenholme Lake district. This loco was scrapped at Crewe Works in January 1985 after sustaining accident damage. Taken in May 1982.

The Advanced Passenger Train (APT), unit No. 370007 (GW), at Glasgow Central having just arrived on a service from London Euston. Unfortunately these units only had a short term in service due to various technical issues. Part of one unit has been kept for the public near Crewe station as a heritage attraction. Taken in June 1984.

No. 47211 (HA) at Mossend Yard with a football special from Aberdeen to King's Park Glasgow. This was provided for Aberdeen supporters to Hampden Park for the Scottish Cup final against Celtic. Aberdeen won the match 2-1. Taken in May 1984.

Eastfield depot on the north side of Glasgow, with classes 08, 25 and 37. This depot was closed in 1996. It was reopened ten years later as a fuelling point and servicing facility for ScotRail diesel units. Taken in May 1984.

Six-car 116/107 DMU combination at Ferguslie Park, near Elderslie, with ECS Corkerhill CSD–Glasgow Central via Elderslie and Paisley Gilmour Street. The ECS were routed this way between May and October 1984 because Corkerhill depot was being electrified. Note the track being lifted in the foreground. This is not far from Paisley Canal where houses were later built over the track bed. This area is now a cycle pathway. Taken in May 1984.

DMU 101360 (ED) descends Cowlairs incline towards Glasgow Queen Street. In the background is a Class 47 with Mk3 coaches climbing up towards Cowlairs. The flats on the right were demolished in 2011. Taken in October 1984.

No. 37039 (ED) emerges out of the gloom
of Glasgow Queen Street Tunnel with the
12.20 service to Oban. This line is scheduled for
electric traction from December 2016. Taken in
October 1984.

No. 37190 (ED) with Class 25 Ethel No. 2 (ex-No. 25268) at Glasgow Queen Street Platform 5. The Ethel was
a converted Class 25, configured to provide electric heating to coaching stock when Class 37 non-ETH locos
were in use. Taken in February 1985.

No. 37267 (ML) at Greenock Central with an advertised day excursion from Gourock to Oban. This loco had recently been transferred to Motherwell from Eastfield depot. It was renumbered as 37421 in January 1986 and reallocated to Inverness depot. This loco was later preserved and is at Bo'ness. Taken in April 1985.

Nos 20110 and 20100 (both ED) at Paisley Gilmour Street with a freight train from MOD Bishopton to Mossend Yard. This MOD facility finally closed in the early 1990s. Taken in September 1986.

No. 154001 (HQ) at Stirling on an Aberdeen–Glasgow Queen Street service. This was the first trial run of a Sprinter to replace Class 47s and Mk2 stock. Eventually, these services were later taken over by Class 158 and 170 units. Taken in March 1987.

No. 47550 (ED) *University Of Dundee* arrives at Stirling with the 12.30 Glasgow Queen Street–Inverness service. This loco was named at Dundee station in May 1982. Taken in May 1987.

No. 31324 (CD) at Glasgow Central with the 13.10 service to Carlisle via Kilmarnock and Dumfries. These locos did not normally work Scottish services but, due to the failure of a Class 27, it was used as the service was booked to be worked by a Carlisle Kingmoor-based driver. This loco was scrapped at Booth Roe Metals, Rotherham, by May 1994. Taken in July 1988.

Corkerhill depot on the south side of Glasgow: from left to right, Class 156, Class 101, Class 107 and a hired-in Class 108, all awaiting their next turn of duty. This depot was electrified in 1984. It now has an allocation of forty-eight two-car Class 156 Sprinters. It also cleans and detanks Class 314 and 380 electric units. Taken in April 1989.

HST at Paisley Gilmour Street with an advertised day excursion from Nottingham to Gourock. Presumably some of the passengers on the train were also sailing to Dunoon from Gourock or, as Glaswegians would say, 'Doon the watter'. Taken in April 1989.

No. 59104 (HQ) near Abington with a test train from Mossend Yard to Carlisle Kingmoor Yard. The loco spent time around Ayrshire on test runs before returning south. This was a prelude to the later Class 66 invasion from General Motors of America. Taken in July 1991.

A three-car 107 at Holytown station with an Edinburgh–Glasgow Central service. At this time this was only an hourly service. The 107s were later replaced by Class 156 units from September 1992 and the service is now half-hourly and worked by a mixture of Class 156 and 158 units. Taken in September 1991.

No. 86242 (WN) approaches Carluke with a Glasgow Central–Manchester express. Carluke now enjoys a half-hourly service to and from Glasgow Central High Level. Taken in July 1991.

No. 320318 (GW) at Drumgelloch (old). This station was reopened in 1989 but was closed in 2010 and replaced by a new double platform as part of the Airdrie–Bathgate line reopening. The new station was located approximately half a mile east from the location of the old station, and enjoys a fast and frequent service between Edinburgh and Glasgow Queen Street Low Level in both directions. Taken in September 1991.

HST Power Car No. 43081 (NL) leading at Lugton with the 10.10 Edinburgh–Poole via Glasgow Central and Kilmarnock service. This service only ran from May until September 1992. However, diverted HSTs were common over the G&SW throughout the 1990s up until 2002, when Class 221 Voyagers replaced them. Taken in July 1992.

No. 305508 (GW) at Glasgow Central station with a special to Edinburgh. The booked GNER Class 91 had failed, so GNER hired the 305 unit from ScotRail to work the service as far as Edinburgh, where another MK4/Class 91 set took over. Taken in March 1993.

No. 303048 (GW), stabled at Shields depot. This unit was repainted to celebrate the blue train anniversary in 1993 and travelled extensively over most electrified routes within the Strathclyde area. It was originally going to be preserved with the SRPS at Bo'ness but, due to asbestos issues, it would prove too costly and was eventually scrapped. Taken in March 1995.

No. 33109 (SF) *Captain Bill Smith* at Ayr station. This loco, plus No. 33116 (SF) *Hertfordshire Railtours*, were brought up to Ayr to work special trains between Kilmarnock and Dumfries in connection with the blockbuster movie *Mission Impossible*. These trains had special cameras fitted to capture background footage. Taken in April 1995.

This is one of the special trains mentioned. The two Class 33s were positioned in the middle of the train, with three coaches either side of them. Each end coach had a special yellow metal platform added, where a movie camera was positioned. This shot shows the special train near New Cumnock, heading south on a Kilmarnock–Dumfries run. Taken in May 1995.

HST north of Mauchline with a diverted Birmingham–Glasgow Central service. Here it takes the single line towards Annbank. The train then ran via Barassie, Kilwinning and Paisley Gilmour Street, due to single-line constraints north of Kilmarnock. Taken in May 1996.

Six-car 325, with unit 003 leading (CE), being loaded with Royal Mail traffic at Glasgow Central station Platform 12. This traffic was transferred to Shieldmuir mail distribution depot south of Motherwell in 2004. Taken in December 1996.

Six-car 303 at Gailes, south of Irvine, with a golf special returning from Troon to Glasgow Central. The 303s generally only worked to the Ayrshire area on specials or if 318 availability was poor. Taken in July 1997.

No. 156432 (CK) at Westerton station. The 156 was being used vice electric traction, a reaction to engineering works taking place in this area. Apparently, the locals preferred the direct service to Glasgow Queen Street High Level. Taken in July 1995.

No. 101304 (ED) at Glasgow Queen Street, having just arrived on a service from Falkirk Grahamston. The unit is about to receive fitters' attention. Many a DMU came to a halt in the tunnel due to the steep 1-in-40 uphill gradient out of Queen Street towards Cowlairs. Taken in May 1990.

No. 47553 (CD) at Muirhouse Junction with a Carlisle–Glasgow Central service. This junction was later renamed Muirhouse North Junction. This is where the Glasgow–Cathcart Circle lines split away from the main diesel lines to Barrhead and Kilmarnock. Taken in May 1986.

No. 47636 (IS) departs Glasgow Central with a Carlisle service via Kilmarnock. Note all the mail bags in the foreground – again, a thing of the past. Taken in February 1986.

Grangemouth depot with Class 20s and Class 37s out based from Eastfield depot. This depot closed in 1989. However, there is still a lot of rail activity around Grangemouth, with Malcolm Rail and others still making use of Grangemouth as a rail terminal point for rail-to-road distribution. Taken in May 1984.

Hamilton depot with classes 107/116 and 121 railcars. This depot provided all diesel traction for the Glasgow Central–Edinburgh via Shotts, for Largs, Ardrossan and Kilmacolm services until it was closed in June 1982. Taken in April 1982.

Gushetfaulds Freightliner depot Glasgow with Class 86s and a Class 08 pilot loco. This was opened in 1965, but was closed in 1989 when all container-based traffic was concentrated at Coatbridge Freightliner terminal. Taken in May 1982.

Greenock Central with a Class 303 EMU and 101 DMU. Due to engineering operations, electric traction could only run from Gourock as far as Greenock Central, where the diesel took over. Taken in May 1984.

Class 303, 314 and Class 37s at Rutherglen station. The electrics are on Argyle line duties and the two Class 37s on the main line are probably heading to Motherwell depot from Hunterston. The line in the foreground connects the Argyle line with the West Coast Main Line, allowing empty coaching stock moves to and from Shields depot for any north electric units requiring maintenance. Taken in September 1980.

No. 140003 (HT) under construction inside Barclay's works, Kilmarnock. These units mainly work in and around the Newcastle area. They have come back to the Kilmarnock works on several occasions for modifications. However, they have not proved popular down south and are scheduled to be withdrawn by 2020. Taken in August 1985.

Prototype Sprinter No. 150001 (DY) at Kilwinning Junction with a Glasgow Central–Stranraer Harbour service. Class 156 units took over these duties from October 1988. The signal box was removed when the Ayrshire electrification programme came in. Taken in February 1986.

Glasgow Underground trains Nos 5 and 16 at Partick. This station is connected to ScotRail's services above by escalators. This shot was on the first day of the reopened underground service, which had closed down for refurbishment from 1977. Taken in May 1980.

No. 303045 (HY) arrives at Glasgow Central Low Level station with a Motherwell–Dalmuir service. The Argyle line was reopened in November 1979. Taken in May 1980.

No. 303055 (HY) at High Street station with an Airdrie–Helensburgh Central limited stopping service. This was the last 303 unit to retain Caledonian blue livery until 1969. Taken in April 1980.

Class 303s galore at Gourock station. This station has now been reduced from four to three platforms. It provides boat connections to and from Dunoon. Taken in May 1984.

No. 303032 (GW) in the new Strathclyde orange livery departs from Glasgow Central with a Neilston-bound service via Queen's Park. The two driving trailers, along with a motor coach from unit No. 303023, have been preserved by the SRPS at Bo'ness. Taken in July 1987.

Class 303 and 311 units await their next turn of duty at Helensburgh Central station. Most of the 311 units were withdrawn by 1994 and the 303 units went in 2001. One 303 unit is preserved at the SRPS at Bo'ness and two coaches from No. 311103 are preserved at the Summerlee Heritage Trust near Coatbridge. Taken in May 1987.

Six-car 303, unit 058 leading (GW), at Kilwinning in the snow with the 08.00 Glasgow Central–Ayr service. Due to the bad weather, 318 availability was poor, so the faithful old Class 303s were stepped up to help out. Taken in January 1987.

No. 303037 (HY) at Bellgrove with a Balloch Central–Springburn service. This unit was involved in the fatal Newton crash of 1991 involving unit No. 314203. It was scrapped after the crash. Taken in April 1980.

No. 311110 (HY) at Balloch Central station, having just arrived with a service from Springburn. This station was re-sited to a new location in 1987 and the single-line branch to Balloch Pier was also closed. Taken in May 1986.

No. 311108 (GW) at Paisley St James with a Glasgow Central–Wemyss Bay service. Wemyss Bay is the location for boat connections to and from Rothesay. This unit was involved in a fatal crash with a Class 116 DMU at Pollokshields East in 1974. Taken in September 1980.

Class 104 PC M53461 had recently transferred from Manchester Newton Heath at Glasgow Central Platform 13 and was about to couple up to another three-car unit to form a service to Ayr. Taken in August 1986.

DMU three-car 105/107 combination at Platform 13 Glasgow Central. This particular working had rear power car E51268 in the formation, which had recently been transferred from Norwich to Ayr to help out with DMU shortages. This train was forming a service to Ardrossan Harbour. Taken in July 1986.

Two Class 20s in the snow with an engineer's train near Howwood, south of Johnstone. The engineer's train was getting used in connection with the Ayrshire electrification project. Taken in February 1986.

No. 31212 (SF) at Mauchline was bringing one of the new Class 318 units from York works to Shields depot in Glasgow. This loco was finally scrapped at MC Metals of Glasgow by May 1995. Taken in September 1986.

Three-car 107 at Kilmacolm with the 13.03 service to Glasgow Central. Note the mixed livery of the coaches. This line at one time continued beyond Kilmacolm to Greenock Princess Pier. This was cut back to boat trains only from 1965, and the line to Elderslie was singled from 1973. The all-blue BR livery was brought into use from 1967 and lasted until around 1982. Taken in June 1980.

Three-car 107 departs Glasgow Central with the 14.12 service to East Kilbride. Note the incorrect headcode '1S07' above the driver's windscreen. This should have been blank or four zeros. Taken in May 1986.

Paisley Gilmour Street sees a Class 318 on the 08.30 Glasgow–Ayr service, while a Class 81 is arriving with the 07.45 Ayr–London Euston via Glasgow Central service. The Class 81 would be replaced by a Class 86 or 87 at Glasgow Central. Taken in June 1987.

No. 86235 *Novelty* (WN) passes Rutherglen old station with a Glasgow Central–Liverpool Lime Street train. The new Rutherglen station was reopened as part of the Argyle line in November 1979 and is behind the camera. Taken in September 1980.

Six-car 126 at Johnstone: power car No. 51012 (AY) leads with a Glasgow Central–Ayr train. The end gangways on these units started to be removed in October 1979; the removal was completed by March 1981. Taken in June 1980.

Three-car 116 DMU at Stevenston No. 1 signal box with a Glasgow Central–Largs working. Note the 'GG Transclyde' symbol along the side of the first coach. The Class 116s were based at Hamilton for the bulk of their time in Scotland. Taken in April 1982.

No. 47712 (HA) *Lady Diana Spencer* at Shotts station with a diverted Edinburgh–Glasgow Central service. This service was diverted via Shotts because of engineering works in the Linlithgow area. Taken in April 1982.

HST at Beattock Summit with a London King's Cross–Edinburgh service diverted due to engineering works on the East Coast Main Line in the Grantshouse area. Taken in February 1985.

No. 25066 (ED) near Cumnock with the 09.25 Sunday empty newspaper vans from Glasgow Central to Manchester Red Bank depot. Newspapers are another traffic flow that the railway has lost to both road and air. This traffic stopped in the early 1990s. Taken in September 1985.

No. 87032 (WN) departs Glasgow Central with a London Euston-bound service. This loco was later named *Kenilworth*. Taken in July 1976.

Six-car 320, with unit 301 (GW) trailing, at Partick with an Airdrie–Helensburgh Central service. These units were in Strathclyde orange from their introduction. The maroon-and-cream livery took over from 2001. From 2011, the new navy-blue ScotRail livery was introduced. Taken in October 2002.

No. 303032 (GW) at Partick with a Dalmuir–Motherwell via Singer and Blantyre service. This unit finished in service with ScotRail in this livery; part of it has been preserved by the SRPS at Bo'ness. Taken in October 2002.

No. 322482 (GW) in the old Platform 11A at Glasgow Central awaits its next turn of duty. These units were transferred to ScotRail in 2001 from North Western trains to cover the Edinburgh–North Berwick service. They were temporarily transferred away to storage in 2004 in reaction to a legal wrangle between ScotRail and the government. They were brought back again in 2005 and refurbished at Barclay's works in Kilmarnock. They remained in service mainly on the North Berwick services until being displaced by the newer Class 380 units in 2011. They were then transferred down to Northern Rail in 2011. Taken in November 2002.

No. 318259 (GW) at Neilston. Normally 318s were not diagrammed to and from Neilston but, due to a 314 failure, this unit was stepped up. 334 units have also worked to Neilston because of 314 failures. Taken in November 2002.

No. 314202 (GW) departs Glasgow Central with a Cathcart Circle service. This was one of the last to survive in the Strathclyde orange livery. Cathcart services run one an hour via Queen's Park and one via Maxwell Park. Taken in October 2003.

No. 67026 (TO) at Carstairs with a northbound parcels train from Crewe to Shieldmuir near Motherwell. Taken in March 2004.

No. 318252 (GW) arrives at Hamilton Central with a Motherwell–Dalmuir service. Taken in March 2004.

No. 156501 (CK) at Uddingston station with an Edinburgh–Glasgow Central via Shotts service. From 2013, this service was also worked by Class 158 units as well. Taken in March 2004.

No. 318251 (GW) at Wemyss Bay, having just arrived on a service from Glasgow Central. This station has been reduced from three to two platforms since 1987. Taken in May 2004.

No. 318264 (GW) at Larkhall, having just arrived on a service from Dalmuir. The Larkhall branch was reconnected to the rail network in December 2005. Taken in July 2006.

No. 158741 (HA) arrives at Maryhill with a Glasgow Queen Street–Anniesland service. This particular stretch of track was very busy between March and August 2016 due to all Edinburgh–Glasgow Queen Street services being diverted over it. Taken in July 2006.

No. 170421 (HA) at Eastfield sidings in Glasgow. This depot closed in 1996 but was reopened as a stabling point with fuelling and cleaning facilities in 2006. Note the side vinyls to promote the forthcoming commonwealth games. Taken in March 2007.

No. 158714 (IS) arrives at Cumbernauld with a Glasgow Queen Street–Falkirk Grahamston service. Taken in March 2007.

No. 66411 (DRS) at Motherwell with the Daventry–Grangemouth Tesco train. This normally runs from Mondays to Fridays. Taken in March 2007.

No. 66192 (TO) at Bank Junction, north of New Cumnock, with a northbound loaded MGR from Greenburn to Ratcliffe power station. This train would reverse in the Long Lye sidings, Kilmarnock, before heading south. Taken in April 2009.

No. 170470 (HA) arrives at Glasgow Queen Street with a service from Dunblane. This station was closed between March and August 2016 for electrification work in connection with the EGIP project that should see Class 380s running initially between Glasgow Queen Street and Edinburgh. In the long term, it is envisaged that brand-new Class 385 units made by Hitachi will replace them from December 2017. Taken in May 2009.

Glasgow Queen Street High Level with Nos 158868 (HA) and 158733 (HA), both ready to depart with their next workings. Taken in May 2009.

No. 158722 (IS) arrives in Glasgow Queen Street with a service from Falkirk Grahamston. This unit was originally allocated to Edinburgh Haymarket in 1989, but has been an Inverness-based unit since 2004. Taken in May 2009.

No. 334008 (GW) at Port Glasgow with a Gourock–Glasgow Central service. Gourock now enjoys four trains per hour to Glasgow Central from 07.00 until 19.00. Taken in November 2009.

Six-car 334, unit 016 (GW) leading, arrives at Airdrie with an Edinburgh–Helensburgh Central service. Taken in May 2011.

No. 156436 (CK) arrives at Hawkhead, near Paisley Canal, with the 13.05 Paisley Canal–Glasgow Central service. Class 314 and 380 Electrics replaced these units from December 2012. Taken in June 2011.

No. 380016 (GW) at Howwood with a Glasgow Central–Largs service. Howwood station was reopened in March 2001. Taken in July 2011.

No. 318252 (GW) at Rutherglen with a Dalmuir–Larkhall service. Note the new M74 motorway bridge overhead. This was opened in 2010. Taken in August 2011.

No. 318269 (GW) at Lanark, having just arrived on a service from Milngavie. Lanark now enjoys a half-hourly service to and from Glasgow Central High Level, worked by a mixture of classes 318, 320 and 380. Taken in August 2011.

No. 380105 (GW) near Hillington West with a Glasgow Central–Ayr service. Note in the background the stations at both Hillington East and Cardonald. The new mid-road was opened in 2012. This was in connection with the proposed link to Glasgow airport that never happened. Taken in March 2012.

No. 66712 (GB) at Cardonald with a Drax–Hunterston empty MGR. This traffic ceased from March 2016. Taken in March 2012.

No. 66249 (TO) at Paisley Gilmour Street with a Hunterston–Longannet loaded MGR train. Taken in March 2012.

No. 380011 (GW) at Bishopton with a Gourock–Glasgow Central service. Taken in March 2012.

No. 156462 (CK) at Kennishead with a Glasgow Central–Barrhead service. Taken in March 2012.

No. 318263 (GW) approaches Dalmuir with a Balloch–Springburn service. Taken in May 2012.

No. 318257 (GW) at Bearsden with a Milngavie–Motherwell service. Taken in May 2012.

No. 334029 (GW) approaches Blackridge with an Edinburgh–Milngavie service. Blackridge reopened in December 2010 as part of the extended Airdrie–Bathgate new service. Taken in June 2012.

No. 380114 (GW) at Cathcart station with the 08.15 Inner Circle service from Glasgow Central. Most of these services are worked by Class 314s, with the 380s working during the morning peak and also usually during football events at Hampden Park. Taken in June 2012.

No. 158728 (HA) at Whifflet with the 10.36 service to Glasgow Central. Diesels on this service were replaced by electric traction from December 2014. Taken in June 2012.

No. 334018 (GW) at Caldercruix with a Helensburgh Central–Edinburgh working. All Class 334s started life in the Strathclyde maroon-and-cream livery, but they are all now all in navy-blue ScotRail saltire colours. Taken in June 2012.

No. 66003 (TO) at Milliken Park with a Longannet–Hunterston empty MGR service. Milliken Park has a half-hourly service to and from Glasgow Central. This station was reopened in 1987. Taken in November 2012.

No. 314209 (GW) at Paisley Canal, having just arrived with the 14.12 service from Glasgow Central. Houses were built over the track bed, making it difficult, but not impossible, to relay the track to Kilmacolm. Taken in April 2012.

No. 156435 (CK) at Priesthill & Darnley station, working the 14.56 Barrhead–Glasgow Central service. This station was reopened in April 1990. Taken in January 2013.

Network Rail HST measuring train at Carstairs heading north from the Derby Research Centre to various Strathclyde locations. Taken in March 2013.

No. 156493 (CK) arrives at Giffnock station with an East Kilbride–Glasgow Central service. Taken in March 2013.

No. 380007 (GW) at Fort Matilda with the 10.04 Gourock–Glasgow Central service. Fort Matilda got its name from a fortress dating from 1814, which was set up to protect the harbour at Greenock. The site is now occupied by naval buildings. Taken in April 2013.

No. 380017 (GW) emerges out of Newton Street tunnel into Greenock West station on the 10.24 Gourock–Glasgow Central service. The tunnel is one of the longest in Scotland, being almost 2 miles in length. Taken in April 2013.

No. 170455 (HA) at Croy with an Edinburgh–Glasgow Queen Street service. These units will eventually be replaced by Class 385 Hitachis from December 2017. Taken in May 2013.

No. 170414 (HA) at Lenzie on an express from Edinburgh to Glasgow Queen Street. Taken in May 2013.

No. 66735 (GB) at Gartcosh with the Fort William–Blyrth Alcan tank train. This takes aluminium from Fort William Rio Tinto factory for use down south. Taken in May 2013.

No. 66150 (TO) near West Kilbride with a Hunterston–Longannet loaded MGR working. Hunterston now has a worrying future since the coal decline from 2015. Taken in October 2013.

No. 318254 (GW) at Hillfoot with a Motherwell–Milngavie service. Services on this branch have suffered a similar fate as the Kilmarnock–Barrhead line due to single-line constraints. This unit crashed through the buffers at Largs in 1995 and was later rebuilt. Taken in November 2013.

No. 156442 (CK) at Shilford Summit, south of Barrhead with a Glasgow Central–Kilmarnock service. This single line still causes congestion when any late running occurs. Taken in April 2014.

No. 66021 (TO) at Kilwinning with a loaded MGR train from Hunterston–Longannet. Taken in April 2014.

No. 334002 (GW) at Yoker Yard between duties. These units usually clock up approximately 300 to 400 miles on average when working. Note the non-multi-sticker X on the non-driver's side windscreen, which indicates that unit is unable to couple up to other 334 units until a fault is fixed by maintenance staff. Taken in May 2014.

No. 334004 (GW) at Garscadden with an Edinburgh–Helensburgh Central service. This service is half-hourly and is one of the longest suburban journeys in the United Kingdom, taking 2 hours end to end. Taken in May 2014.

No. 156478 (CK) arrives in Glasgow Central Platform 3 with a train from East Kilbride. This unit was damaged by flooding near Mauchline in January 2015 while it was working a Glasgow Central–Carlisle service. It presently languishes at Brodies Works in Kilmarnock and looks likely to be scrapped. Taken in May 2014.

No. 66177 (TO) at Ballieston with an empty MGR from Longannet to Hunterston. This service was operated by DBS, although Freightliner Heavy Haul have also ventured into Ayrshire as well. Taken in May 2014.

No. 66060 (TO) approaches Cumbernauld with a loaded MGR from Hunterston to Longannet. Taken in May 2014.

No. 334022 (GW) approaches Greenfaulds with a Dalmuir–Cumbernauld service. This unit was repainted at Brodies of Kilmarnock in 2013. Taken in May 2014.

No. 158732 (HA) at Stepps with the 10.18 Glasgow Queen Street–Falkirk Grahamston service. Taken in May 2014.

No. 318269 (GW) at High Street with a Cumbernauld–Dalmuir service. Taken in May 2014.

Six-car 334, unit 016 (GW) leading, at Shettleston with an Edinburgh–Milngavie working. Taken in May 2014.

Six-car 320, unit 310 leading (GW), arrives at Blairhill with an Airdrie–Balloch train. Taken in May 2014.

No. 320321 (GW) at Duke Street with a Dalmuir–Cumbernauld service. Taken in May 2014.

No. 380102 (GW) at Partick with an Anniesland–Rutherglen service. 380 units are not normally used on the north electric system. Due to extra capacity requirements in connection with the 2014 Commonwealth Games, four units were drafted in to strengthen the already busy services. Taken in July 2014.

No. 92038 (CE) near Crawford with an engineer's train from Carlisle Kingmoor Yard to Millerhill Yard near Edinburgh. Taken in August 2014.

Virgin Pendolino at Abington with a northbound passenger service from London Euston to Glasgow Central. This service is now running at hourly intervals. Taken in August 2014.

Nos 86613/606 (BOTH FLT) at Abington with the 14.14 Coatbridge–Crewe Freightliner service. These locos were introduced in 1965 and are still running strong today. Taken in August 2014.

No. 318254 (GW) at Renton with an Airdrie–Balloch service. The Balloch branch was singled in the late 1970s. Taken in September 2014.

Six-car 320, unit 313 (GW) leading, arrives at Dumbarton East with a Balloch–Airdrie service. Taken in September 2014.

Six-car 318/320 combination, unit 268 leading (GW), at Bowling with an Airdrie–Balloch service. Note the Erskine Road Bridge in the background. Taken in September 2014.

No. 66069 (TO) at Mount Vernon with a tank train heading from Mossend Yard to Irvine Caledonian Pulp Mill. Taken in November 2014.

No. 158739 (HA) at Shotts station with an Edinburgh–Glasgow Central service. These units initially worked Edinburgh–Glasgow Queen Street services but can now be seen virtually anywhere in the Strathclyde area. Taken in November 2014.

Six-car 320, unit 301 leading (GW), arriving at Bellshill with a Dalmuir–Motherwell service. Note the gradient approaching Bellshill. This gradient used to be a stiff test for any heavy freights but electrics just whizz up it. Taken in November 2014.

No. 170401 (HA) at Cowlairs South Junction with a Falkirk Grahamston–Glasgow Queen Street service. Taken in November 2014.

No. 156436 (CK) near Hairmyres with an East Kilbride–Glasgow Central service. Taken in July 2015.

No. 60002 (CL) near New Cumnock with a Dalston–Grangemouth tank train. This train had been diverted away from WCML due to Lamington viaduct being damaged by storm Frank. The WCML was closed from the beginning of January until late February 2016. Taken in January 2016.

Five-car Voyager near Lugton with a diverted Carlisle–Glasgow Central service. This specially diverted service was introduced to provide passengers with a connection at Carlisle for connections further south. However, once again due to the single-line constraints between Barrhead and Kilmarnock, ScotRail were forced to reduce their Kilmarnock–Glasgow Central service to an hourly pattern. Taken in February 2016.

No. 170470 (HA) at Anniesland takes the junction towards Kelvindale with a diverted Glasgow Queen Street Low Level–Edinburgh service. Taken in March 2016.

Six-car 170, unit 395 leading (HA), approaches Anniesland with a diverted Edinburgh–Glasgow Queen Street Low Level service, due to Glasgow Queen Street High level being closed between March and August 2016 for extensive engineering works in connection with electrification of the line and track lowering. Taken in March 2016.

No. 320411 (GW) at Anniesland with a Motherwell–Dalmuir service. This unit was recently transferred to Scotland from the London Midland region. It was previously a four-car unit and classified as a 321. One trailer coach was then removed at Wabtec Doncaster before the unit was brought to Scotland as a reclassified 320 unit. Taken in March 2016.

Glasgow Tram Coronation No. 1297 at Broomielaw next to the Clyde during the Glasgow Garden Festival. The trams finished in Glasgow in 1962; this is the only time that trams have run from then in Glasgow. The track along the Clyde was only approximately a mile and a half in length. The garden festival ran from April until September 1988. Taken in June 1988.